IGUANODON

LEIGH ROCKWOOD

PowerKiDS press™

New York

Published in 2012 by The Rosen Publishing Group, Inc.
29 East 21st Street, New York, NY 10010

First Edition

Editor: Joanne Randolph
Book Design: Kate Laczynski

Photo Credits: Cover, title page by Brian Garvey; cover background (palm tree leaves) © www.iStockphoto.com/dra_schwartz; cover background (palm tree trunk) iStockphoto/Thinkstock; cover background (ginkgo leaves) Hemera/Thinkstock; cover background (fern leaves) Brand X Pictures/Thinkstock; cover background (moss texture) © www.iStockphoto.com/Robert Linton; pp. 4, 20–21 Highlights for Children/Getty Images; p. 5 Louie Psihoyos/Getty Images; p. 6 Andy Crawford/Getty Images; pp. 7, 10, 11, 13, 16, 19 © 2011 Orpheus Books Ltd.; p. 8 © www.iStockphoto.com/Solange Zangiacomo; p. 9 © www.iStockphoto.com/Paul Morton; pp. 12, 22 Colin Keates/Getty Images; p. 14 John Downes/Getty Images; p. 15 Jupiterimages/Photos.com/Thinkstock; p. 17 © www.iStockphoto.com/Ekely; p. 18 Shutterstock.com.

Library of Congress Cataloging-in-Publication Data

Rockwood, Leigh.
   Iguanodon / by Leigh Rockwood. — 1st ed.
       p. cm. — (Dinosaurs ruled!)
   Includes index.
   ISBN 978-1-4488-4974-1 (library binding) — ISBN 978-1-4488-5098-3 (pbk.) —
ISBN 978-1-4488-5099-0 (6-pack)
   1. Iguanodon—Juvenile literature. 2. Paleontology—Cretaceous—Juvenile literature. I. Title. II. Series.
   QE862.O65R6244 2012
   567.914—dc22

2011004465

Manufactured in the United States of America

CPSIA Compliance Information: Batch #WS11PK: For Further Information contact Rosen Publishing, New York, New York at 1-800-237-9932

CONTENTS

MEET THE IGUANODON

When the term "dinosaur" was coined, the iguanodon was one of the three known dinosaurs. "Iguanodon" means "iguana tooth." The dinosaur was given this name because **fossils** of its teeth looked like those of today's iguanas.

Iguanodons had beaklike mouths that they used to eat plants. They are related to hadrosaurs and other dinosaurs that are grouped together based on their teeth.

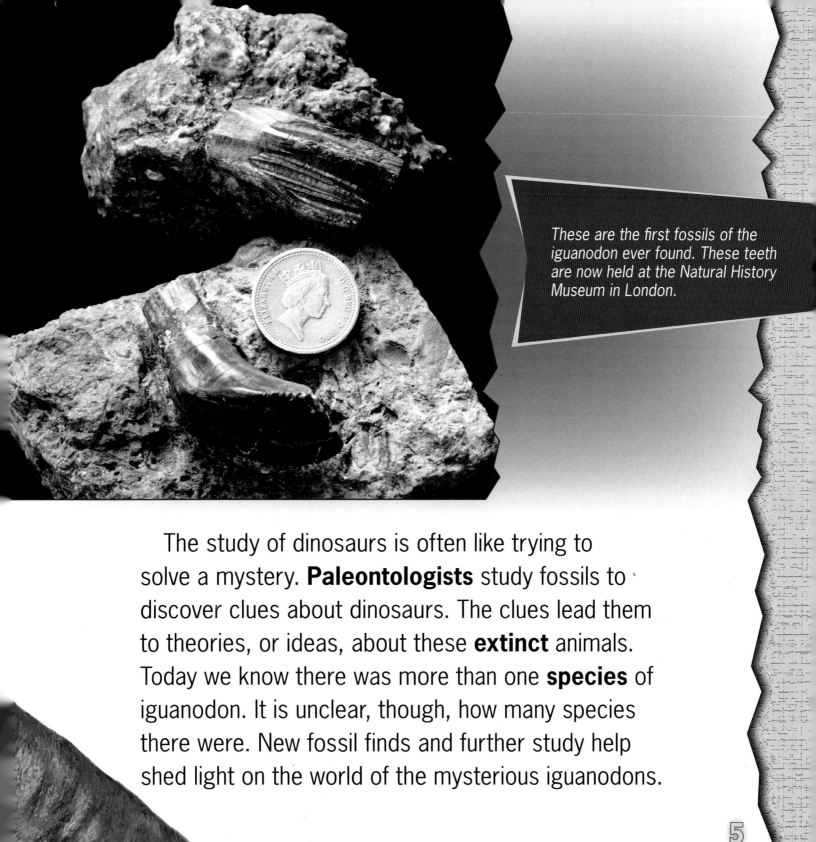

These are the first fossils of the iguanodon ever found. These teeth are now held at the Natural History Museum in London.

The study of dinosaurs is often like trying to solve a mystery. **Paleontologists** study fossils to discover clues about dinosaurs. The clues lead them to theories, or ideas, about these **extinct** animals. Today we know there was more than one **species** of iguanodon. It is unclear, though, how many species there were. New fossil finds and further study help shed light on the world of the mysterious iguanodons.

THE EARLY CRETACEOUS PERIOD

Scientists use a system called geologic time to organize Earth's 4.5-billion-year history. Iguanodons lived during the Early Cretaceous period, which was from around 135 to 125 million years ago. In the Early Cretaceous period, Earth's continents were one giant landmass,

During the Cretaceous period, Earth's landmasses broke apart. Over time they would come together to look more like they do today.

called Pangaea, which was starting to break up into smaller landmasses. This explains why iguanodon fossils have been found on more than one of today's continents.

Dinosaurs became extinct at the end of the Cretaceous period, which was about 65 million years ago. Paleontologists' theories about why dinosaurs died out include asteroids, volcanic activity, and **climate** change.

These are some of the other dinosaurs that lived at the same time as iguanodons. The predators on the lower right are called Yangchuanosauruses.

WHERE DID IGUANODONS LIVE?

Fossils form in **sedimentary rocks**. Sedimentary rocks form when layers of mud, sand, or stone are pressed together. If a plant or animal gets trapped in these layers of sediment, it may become fossilized.

Iguanodon fossils have been found in what are today the European countries of Austria, Belgium, France, Germany, Great Britain, Romania, and Spain as well

Iguanodon fossils have been discovered in South Dakota's Black Hills, in a ridge of sedimentary rocks called the Lakota Formation.

Sedimentary rocks often have a striped look, as these ones do. Each stripe is a layer of sediment that has been pressed and hardened into rock over time.

as in Africa. The most recently discovered iguanodon species was found in South Dakota. It is thought to be one of the oldest known iguanodon species. The places that iguanodon fossils have been found have a wide range of **habitats** and climates today. These places would all have been warm woodlands during the Early Cretaceous period, though.

THE IGUANODON'S BODY

DINO BITE

Paleontologists learned that iguanodons mostly walked on all fours by studying fossilized footprints.

A full-grown iguanodon was between 20 and 30 feet (6–9 m) long and stood 9 feet (3 m) tall at its hips. This dinosaur likely weighed between 4 and 5 tons (4–4.5 t).

The iguanodon had thick, columnlike back legs and thinner front legs. Paleontologists think that these dinosaurs mostly walked on all four legs. They

Iguanodons had large midsections. This is a common feature of plant-eating animals.

As you can see here, one of these iguanodons is standing on four feet, while the other one is standing on its back legs.

also think that their back legs were strong enough to support their whole bodies. That means they could stand on their back legs to reach food. The iguanodon's long tail helped it keep its balance when it stood on its back legs.

11

THUMBS UP!

DINO BITE

Iguanodons may also have used their thumb spikes to open fruits.

The iguanodon had five-fingered hands on its forelimbs. Three fingers were joined together in the middle of each hand. There was also a fourth finger that stuck out to the side and a thumb.

Paleontologists theorize that iguanodons used their three middle fingers to hold food. The fourth finger could move more than the three middle fingers. It likely helped the dinosaurs hold on to things.

This is a fossilized iguanodon hand. You can see the three fingers in the middle, the longer fourth finger at the top, and the thumb spike on the bottom.

Iguanodons may have used their sharp thumb spikes to make predators think twice about eating them. This iguanodon has stabbed an enemy in the neck.

Iguanodons' thumbs had 1-foot-(30 cm) long spikes. These spikes may have been used for **defense** against **predators**. The spikes were large compared to the rest of their hands. Paleontologists once thought the spikes were horns and were attached to their noses rather than their thumbs!

IGUANA TOOTH

As noted before, the iguanodon was named for the fact that it had teeth like an iguana's. Studying an animal's teeth can tell scientists a lot about an animal. It gives them clues about what it ate and if it could bite other animals in defense.

The front of iguanodons' mouths formed toothless, horny beaks. Along each side of their jaws were tightly

A fossilized iguanodon skull, such as this one, can tell a paleontologist a lot about the iguanodon. Do you see the flat teeth that iguanodons used to grind up plants?

Iguanas are large lizards that live in warm, wet places in the wild. Many people also keep iguanas as pets. These lizards gave their name to the prehistoric iguanodon.

spaced teeth, called cheek teeth. The cheek teeth were about 2 inches (5 cm) long. From the placement, size, and shape of its teeth, paleontologists can tell that the iguanodon was a plant eater. Its toothless beak would have broken off pieces of plants and the cheek teeth would have ground them up.

A Plant-Eating Dinosaur

The iguanodon was a plant-eating dinosaur, or an **herbivore**. It likely ate the leaves, shoots, and branches of trees. The trees growing in the dinosaur's Early Cretaceous period habitat included conifers, cycads, and ginkgoes. The iguanodon also likely ate ferns and horsetail plants that grew along rivers.

Iguanodons used their fingers to hold on to plants as they ripped off pieces with their beaklike mouths.

Horsetails grew in wet, swampy places during the Cretaceous period, just as they do today. They have bamboolike stems and feathery leaves.

The iguanodon would have used its horny, turtlelike beak to tear off pieces of trees. The food was then pushed back to the cheek teeth, where the plant material was ground down. The close spacing of these teeth as well as its cheeks would have kept the food from spilling out of its mouth.

ON THE MOVE

Paleontologists learn about how iguanodons moved by studying the length of the dinosaurs' legs as well as their overall size and weight. Heavy animals with short legs tend to move more slowly than lighter, long-legged animals. Scientists can also study fossilized dinosaur footprints. Footprints are farther apart when an animal is running than when it is walking.

Iguanodon tracks, such as these, tell scientists how many dinosaurs were moving together. They can also help tell scientists how fast the dinosaurs moved.

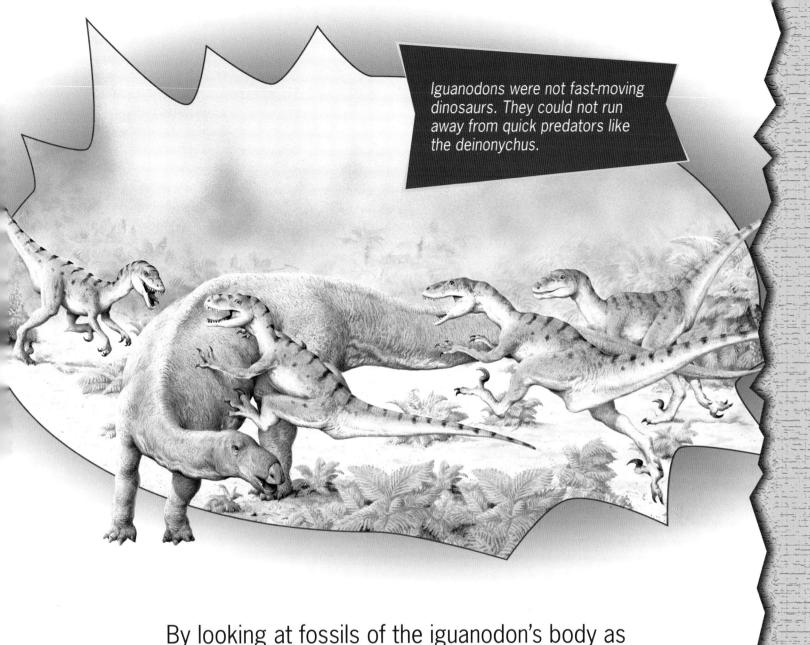

Iguanodons were not fast-moving dinosaurs. They could not run away from quick predators like the deinonychus.

By looking at fossils of the iguanodon's body as well as the spacing between its fossilized footprints, paleontologists can guess how fast the dinosaur could move. They think that iguanodons had a top speed of 9 to 12 miles per hour (15–20 km/h).

IN THE HERD

Iguanodons likely lived in, or at least traveled in, herds. One reason paleontologists think this is because many other plant-eating dinosaurs lived in herds. This may have given herbivores safety in numbers, since there were more eyes to watch out for predators!

The biggest clue that this dinosaur formed herds was the 1878 discovery of the bones from 31 iguanodons in a coal mine in

Here a large herd of iguanodons are shown walking through a swamp.

Belgium. These iguanodons all died together, which led paleontologists to guess that the dinosaurs might have been caught in a flood. The muddy floodwater would have covered the bodies with sediment, which built up over millions of years and formed the fossils.

NO BONES ABOUT IT

The first iguanodon fossil was a tooth found by Gideon Mantell and his wife, Mary Ann Mantell, in 1820 in England. Gideon Mantell was the person who came up with the name iguanodon. He picked it because the tooth he found looked so much like that of an iguana.

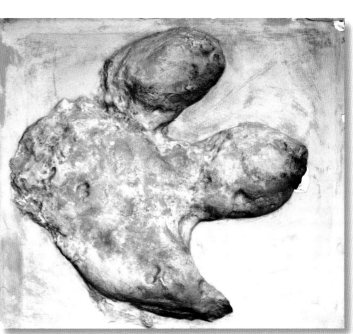

This is a fossil of an iguanodon footprint. Each fossil that is found helps scientists add to what is known about the iguanodon.

Hundreds of iguanodon fossils have been found since the Mantells made their discovery. Because the iguanodon was one of the first dinosaurs discovered, many fossils were mistakenly **classified** as iguanodon and then later changed as paleontologists made new discoveries. This is a good example of how paleontology is a science that never stops changing, even though its subjects have been extinct for millions of years!

GLOSSARY

classified (KLA-seh-fyd) Arranged in groups.

climate (KLY-mut) The kind of weather a certain place has.

defense (dih-FENTS) Something a living thing does that helps keep it safe.

extinct (ik-STINGKT) No longer existing.

fossils (FO-sulz) The hardened remains of dead animals or plants.

habitats (HA-beh-tats) The kinds of land where animals or plants naturally live.

herbivore (ER-buh-vor) An animal that eats only plants.

paleontologists (pay-lee-on-TAH-luh-jists) People who study things that lived in the past.

predators (PREH-duh-terz) Animals that kill other animals for food.

sedimentary rocks (seh-deh-MEN-teh-ree ROKS) Stones, sand, or mud that has been pressed together to form rocks.

species (SPEE-sheez) One kind of living thing. All people are one species.

INDEX

WEB SITES

Due to the changing nature of Internet links, PowerKids Press has developed an online list of Web sites related to the subject of this book. This site is updated regularly. Please use this link to access the list:
www.powerkidslinks.com/dinr/iguano/

ML   11 / 11